M000073391

Hospitality
and the
Holy Spirit

A hotelier's stories and perspective on what
the Bible tells us about taking care of people

Denise Maiatico

© 2020 by Denise Maiatico
All rights reserved. No part of this publication may be reproduced or transmitted in any form or by any means, electronic or mechanical, including photocopying, recording, or any other information storage and retrieval system, without the written permission of the publisher.
Printed in the United States of America
Published in Hellertown, PA
Edited by Jennifer Bright
Proofread by Skye Cruz
Cover and interior design by Bravura Graphics, LLC
Art by Bravura Graphics, LLC
Scripture quotations marked BSB are taken from The Holy Bible, Berean Study Bible, BSB, Copyright ©2016, 2018 by Bible Hub, Used by Permission. All Rights Reserved Worldwide.
Scripture quotations marked CEV are from the Contemporary English Version Copyright © 1991, 1992, 1995 by American Bible Society, Used by Permission.
Scripture quotations marked ESV are taken from The Holy Bible, English Standard Version. ESV® Text Edition: 2016. Copyright © 2001 by Crossway Bibles, a publishing ministry of Good News Publishers.
Scripture quotations marked KJV are taken from the King James Version of the Bible.
Scripture quotations marked NIV are taken from the Holy Bible, New International Version®. niv®. Copyright © 1973, 1978, 1984, 2011 by Biblica, Inc.™ Used by permission. All rights reserved worldwide.
Scripture quotations marked NLT are taken from the Holy Bible, New Living Translation copyright ©1996, 2004, 2007 by Tyndale House Foundation. Used by permission of Tyndale House Publishers, Inc. Carol Stream, Illinois 60188. All rights reserved.
Library of Congress Control Number 2020900692
ISBN 978-0-9994151-5-3
2 4 6 8 10 9 7 5 3 1 paperback

This book is dedicated to everyone who smiles back!
God Bless you!

Denise

Acknowledgements

We all have a story to tell. Thank you to my family, who encouraged me to share mine: my husband, Gary; my daughter, Hope; my mom; my dad and Deb; my brother, Ed; my mother-in-law, Esther; my sister-in-law, Val; and my brother-in-law, Jeff.

Thank you for the heart connections and conversations that helped the words find their way to these pages and the pages fall in order. I'm inspired by Reverend Michael McGowan, Samantha Chitswara, Anne Baum, Jennifer Bright and Momosa Publishing, Terri Tucker, Joe DeVita, Pastor Brandon, Cheyenne Bennett, Beverly Bradley, Tom Jebran, Richard Jabara, William Meyer, Rick Odorisio, Michelle Goad, Pam Rex, Gina Martens, David Schweiger, Rebecca Heid, Joe Posh, Joan Green, Tom Garrity, Matt Kulp, John Yurconic, Andy Montero, Tina Hamilton, Kim Plyler, Buddy Lesavoy, Ben Spalding, Joe Farkas, Keith O'Brien, and Eileen Smith.

Contents

Introduction

What does the Holy Spirit have to do with hospitality? A lot, it turns out. Stories and advice about being a good host abound in the Bible. Some are as well known as the story of Jesus' birth. Others are more obscure, and I enjoyed researching those especially.

Why did I choose to look at the Bible through the lens of hospitality? I'm a hospitality professional. I've spent the past 20 plus years building a career in the hotel business. I manage a variety of upscale hotels. I've seen some crazy, wonderful, disturbing, and inspirational things.

I'm convinced I've been in the presence of both angels and demons on this journey, and I am grateful for the lessons I have learned from both. I'm a Christian who wants to explore the Bible on a deeper level and through the lens of my experiences.

To create this book, I researched Bible stories and married them to my own experiences. During this process, the lessons of the Gospel became both relevant and obvious to me as I considered my personal journey and desire to live a life that reflects hospitality as my purpose as well as my profession.

No Room at the
Inn in Bethlehem

"He took with him Mary, to whom he was engaged, who was
now expecting a child. And while they were there, the time
came for her baby to be born. She gave birth to her firstborn
son. She wrapped him snugly in strips of cloths and laid
him in a manger, because there was no lodging available for
them" (Luke 2:5–7 NLT)

When people think of hospitality in the Bible, this is probably the story that comes to mind. What does this story say about hospitality?

It's a tale of travel at a time when people didn't travel for fun or leisure. Transportation and lodging options were scarce, and travelers often relied on the generosity and hospitality of other people who would take them in and provide shelter and food as they ventured from the safety of their homes. Hospitality at the time of Jesus' birth was a heart-calling. It required a desire and willingness to serve people in need.

When I read this Bible story, I imagine that the next morning, Joseph went on Trip Advisor and posted a negative review about the inn and the heartless innkeeper who had no compassion for their situation and put the life of his family at risk when he turned them away—a one-star rating with photos of the lowly manger where his son spent the first night of his life.

The word "hospitality" is derived from the root word hospice, which translates as "to provide care and shelter for travelers." There are numerous references to hospitality in the Bible. I think about ancient times—when travel was dramatically different than it is today. Back then, it was a scary and uncomfortable endeavor to venture beyond your community. Many people lived and died without exploration beyond the region where they were born. In ancient times, innkeepers were often unsavory and opportunistic criminals who masqueraded as hospitable, but would rob guests as they attempted to sleep in grass- and bug-filled common beds, head-to-toe with other travelers. No doubt they were all anxious and eager to see the light of morning.

One day, 2012 years, 9 months, and 22 days after Mary and Joseph were turned away from the inn on Christmas Eve, I found myself working as the General Manager at a hotel in Bethlehem—Bethlehem, Pennsylvania. I was a world away from the site of the holy birth, but still, I felt the weight of that coincidence. It was a dark and stormy night—very stormy. In fact, we were having a hurricane.

Travelers were stumbling into the inn seeking shelter. The hotel was already full when most of them arrived. There was literally no room at the inn in Bethlehem!

Our team did absolutely everything we could do to serve our guests. We offered fresh towels, hot coffee, healthy nourishing food options, and even some themed hurricane cocktails for the lucky few who had reservations. Many people were turned away. I think about Joseph and Mary. I think about the countless faces young, old, scared, maybe even pregnant who stumbled back out into the storm that night. We were in touch with every hotel within an hour's drive and attempted to direct each guest to an available room. I wonder where they slept, if they slept. I wonder if I was the best manager, leader, and Christian I could have been. Was I following the hospitality principles the Bible taught me?

Let me be perfectly clear: I work in a for-profit world. I've built a career generating a financial return for hotel owners and balancing demand through a formula of driving occupancy and rates. Give to Caesar the things that are Caesar's. (Matthew 22:21) I don't want you to think that my inner thoughts make me a missionary who has dedicated her life to feeding the poor.

Although I enjoy volunteering and serving others, my work is focused on serving paying guests, developing associates, and generating a financial return for owners. I'd like to think if you spoke with these customer groups, they'd say I'm good at what I do. I like my work. I find both challenge and reward in this industry. The fascinating people I meet have certainly led to a collection of stories worth sharing.

"It's not what you do. It's how you do it." I'm sure you've seen a plaque somewhere with these words. I believe this statement. I believe I can be great at my job and live as an example of a woman seeking Christ and behaving in a way that reflects my values. That all sounds very serious, but "there is a time to dance," and it would be impossible to serve the public for 20 years without a sense of humor and desire to have some fun. I hope as you read the following chapters, you'll take a trip with me through the hospitality lessons of the Bible and their application to our modern world.

Together, we can make the connections. We can continue our pursuit of hospitality—with a dose of inspiration from the Holy Spirit.

Dear Lord, Help me to be a refuge for others. Help my thoughts and behaviors be a reflection of service and hospitality. I pray that the Holy Spirit is alive in me and keeps me from selfish or stupid thoughts or actions. Amen.

Angels Are All Around

"Do not neglect to show hospitality to strangers, for thereby
some have entertained angels unawares." (Hebrews 13:2 ESV)

This Bible story literally says the word "hospitality." What does this do to illuminate the Biblical perspective on hospitality?

Hospitality is demonstrated in moments. It's about the decision made in a momentary encounter with a stranger. Do you pause, connect, offer a greeting? Or do you simply continue on your way? We miss so many opportunities to show hospitality. The Biblical stories of hospitality are telling us to slow down, look up, and connect with and serve others. That is the core concept of hospitality.

I find myself captivated by the accounts of angels in the Bible. In an effort to understand their role, I researched angel encounters. The Bible tells us that God created angels. That may sound simple, and more information about their creation is important to me as I attempt to understand the role of an angel—in particular the one I met.

Paul tells us that God created all things visible and invisible, so this includes angels. Angels appear in the Bible in three types.

Cherubim are the first angel type. They guarded the entrance to the Garden of Eden (Genesis 3:24), and they also sit above the Arc of the Covenant as expressed in Exodus 25:22.

The second type of angel, seraphim, are mentioned in Isaiah 6:2-7. They continually worship the Lord and sing of His praises.

It's the third type of angel that I truly wanted to understand: the angels who appear as living creatures or in human form. Revelation speaks of heavenly beings that appeared "like a lion, the second like a calf, the third had the face of a man, and the fourth was an eagle in flight... Day and night they never stop saying, 'Holy, holy, holy is the Lord God Almighty, who was and is and is to come!'" (Revelation 4:7–8 BSB) In the book *Angels in the Bible: What Do We Actually Know About Them?* Wayne Grudem describes attributes of angels: They do not marry, they are very powerful, they are an example for us, they carry out some of God's plans, they directly glorify God, and they are not to be worshiped.

My favorite example of an angel in human form from the Bible is found in Genesis. We meet Joseph, the second youngest of 12 brothers, 17 years old, with a coat that was a special gift from his father and more colorful and beautiful than the trendiest attire that graces today's fashion week runways. He was his father's favorite. If you have a brother, like I do, you can only imagine the conflict and chaos that could erupt from a clan of 12 boys, especially when everyone knows one of them is getting special attention and gifts from his father.

As the story goes, Joseph had dreams that appear to allude to a day when his brothers would bow down to him. I've been known to get myself whipped up if my brother beats me at a game of Uno, so I can only imagine how the interpretation of Joseph's dreams sent the older brothers into a fury. In Genesis 37:14, Joseph's brothers had taken the sheep out to pasture. Joseph's father, Jacob, asked him to "Go and find out how your brothers and the sheep are doing. Then come back and let me know." (Genesis 37:14 CEV)

That sounds like a simple assignment, but this is where it gets interesting. Joseph sets out to the pasture where his brothers were headed, but he ends up wandering through the fields and cannot find them. We don't really know how long he wandered, if he was truly and completely lost, if he was scared, or if he was just enjoying an afternoon strutting around in his beautiful coat. What we do know is that he wasn't able to find his brothers.

If you know the story, you know that Joseph is destined for an amazing journey—one of hardship, discovery, and triumph that will cement his faith in God and become an amazing testimony to prisoners, Pharaoh, and his own family. But at this point in the story, he's wandering. The whole story would have fallen apart if Joseph hadn't connected with and gotten betrayed by his brothers. Suddenly, in the middle of a pasture, a man appears and asks, "What are you looking for?" (Genesis 37:15)

I find the appearance of this man, just at the time when Joseph needed guidance and direction, very intriguing.

We could speculate that this man wasn't just a man, but an angel in human form who interceded to make sure Joseph completed the important step on his journey where he connected with his brothers near Shechem.

As the story continues, Joseph meets his brothers, who had been plotting his demise. They decide not to kill him. Instead, they sell him to a passing caravan, and they lie to their father about what happened. The caravan then sells Joseph to the Ishmaelites, who then sell him to Potiphar in Egypt. Potiphar is the king's official in charge of the palace guard. When Joseph refuses the advances of Potiphar's wife, she accuses him of rape, and he ends up in jail with Pharaoh's cupbearer.

While Joseph is in jail, he interprets a dream of the cupbearer. Years later, Pharaoh has a dream he can't understand. The cupbearer, who has since been released from prison, tells Pharaoh of Joseph and his unique ability to interpret dreams. Pharaoh summons Joseph, who gives insight into Pharaoh's dream, giving God full credit for his ability to interpret dreams. Joseph explains the dream was giving God's warning of seven years without any resources. He also gives the gift of a solution: Store extra supplies for the next seven years in preparation for the bad years.

Pharaoh believed Joseph and put him in charge of all of the land of Egypt. Joseph was now in charge of selling all grain in Egypt.

Joseph's brothers journeyed to Egypt to buy grain. This was 10 years after they had sold Joseph. Ironically, Joseph was now in charge of selling the grain they wanted to buy. The brothers bowed down to

Joseph, as he had seen in his dream. Joseph revealed himself to them and forgave them for their ill intentions. He knew God had put him there to stop people from starving.

Everything that happened to Joseph was an essential and connected part of the journey that would reveal the glory of God and his true calling.

Joseph's brothers and their father ended up moving to Egypt to live with Joseph, and they had all the food they needed.

It certainly was fortunate for all of them—and in fact for all of the Egyptians—that Joseph didn't get lost and continue wandering in the pasture that day when his father sent him to check on his brothers and the sheep. How fortunate it was that the mysterious man appeared, unexpectedly and out of nowhere, to guide Joseph in the right direction to fulfill his destiny.

Metaphorically, have you ever been a bit lost? Wandering? On the wrong path? Not connecting with something important that will help to determine your future? Do you believe in angels who can take human form and help us find our way?

I was lost once—in Providence, Rhode Island.

I began my hotel career in the food and beverage side of the business, setting up promotions, dressing up in costumes to match happy hour–themed buffets, and marketing our busy night clubs. I was good at it, not because I'm super talented, but because it was incredibly fun! After a short time, I transitioned to event planning and sales, which was also fun, but a much more respected and professional position.

My results caught the attention of some of our executives, and I was invited to attend an executive session. Some people dream of attending the Oscars or the Royal Wedding. Me? I dreamed of attending an executive session.

This was where owners and general managers convened for three days to determine strategic direction for our properties, learn about emerging trends, eat ridiculously expensive meals, and establish themselves as the best and brightest in our company and the industry.

Willy Wonka has his golden tickets. My company has invitations to the annual executive session, and I received one.

Of course, I did what any young lady determined to make her mark would do. I bought three new outfits. The truth is that I really couldn't afford them, but you only get one chance, right? And I was not going to blow it.

That year's executive session was held at the Marriott in Providence, Rhode Island. I traveled five hours to the hotel. After I arrived, I gathered every bit of confidence to walk through the revolving doors, across the marble tile, and into the event that I was sure would determine my future. Raving success or abysmal failure—everything rested on the next 54 hours of my life.

I checked into the hotel. My guest room was spectacular. On the credenza sat a basket full of amenities, snacks, gifts, and a personalized welcome note. I was in hotel heaven and loving it.

I set multiple alarms and confirmed a wake-up call. I attempted to get some sleep and dream about what day one of the session would bring.

The next morning, the worst possible thing that my naïve mind could have imagined happened. When I woke up, I tried to look at the clock to check the time. But I couldn't open my eyes. They were glued shut, caked with a disgusting, dried, oozy coating.

I thought, *Are you kidding me? Not here! Not now!*

I knew immediately what it was—pink eye.

If you've never had pick eye, you should know:

• It's disgusting.

• It's contagious.

• The drops that you get from the doctor are the closest thing to a miracle drug that I've ever experienced. As soon as you put the drops into your effected eye, improvement begins. But pink eye doesn't clear up on its own. Without the drops, you'll just get more disgusting ooze.

My new morning mission was to get my hands on some pink eye prescription eyedrops ASAP. At the sacrifice of quite a few eyelashes, I pried my eyes open and softened the crust with hot water. I could now see to find the phone.

I called the front desk, desperate for a doctor who would see me quickly and without question to dispense the much-desired drops. The attendant at the front desk politely informed me that it was 6 am. The only option was to go to the emergency department at the local hospital. She explained that the hotel shuttle was available, and it would be their pleasure to provide transportation.

Clad in my $15 sweats with my hair still unbrushed, I bounded to the lobby and into the van. I'm sure the driver was friendly, but that's not how I remember him. I pleaded with him to wait for me at the curb because I was only going to be a minute. I just needed to grab the drops and get back to the hotel for my very important meeting. He informed me he wasn't able to idle at the curb and that I should call him when I was ready to be picked up, and he would return then. He probably knew that this wasn't going to be a quick in-and-out visit. Honestly, have you ever had a quick visit to an emergency department?

I entered the waiting area, and to my delight, it was empty. There wasn't a soul to be found—no bleeding or vomiting patients, only me with my sticky eyes. I was thrilled, thinking I'd be in and out in no time. Maybe this disaster of a day could be turned around, maybe the worst possible thing I could have ever imagined didn't just happen, maybe my illustrious career could still play out, maybe I could have it all—the great job, pretty clothes, beautiful house, adoring husband, and shiny new sports car.

I approached the receptionist with urgency and a lack of patience, talking rapidly to express my self-diagnosis and desire to very quickly be given the drops so my life could get back on track. She put me in my place by asking me to sign the sheet and take a seat until they called me.

I have no idea how long I sat there. Every minute of waiting seemed to turn up the heat in my bloodstream and toss paint thinner on the portrait of my future dreams. Have you ever felt that way? Like suddenly the tide was against you and you are the victim of an evil plot of the universe that's determined to destroy you? I know that sounds dramatic, and it is, but I was young and had led a fairly charmed life. I was blissfully, selfishly unaware of the reality of struggle and pain in the world. I was wandering in the pasture. I was walking around in a pretty coat, but I was truly quite lost.

After some time in the waiting room, like a scene from *Cops*, the emergency department doors flew open, and a gurney rolled in, filling the space with chaos. Doctors and nurses appeared out of thin air and rushed to the scene.

Strapped to the bed was the most disgusting man I've ever seen. He was filthy dirty—from the couple of greasy hairs that stuck to the top of his head to the soles of his feet. I can still picture him thrashing back and forth against the restraints, as fluids spewed from his nose and mouth, the sweat from his pores working hard to find its way through the caked-on dirt.

At that moment, one thought crossed my mind, *Oh great, he's definitely going to get in and be seen before me.*

I was right. As they rolled the man out of sight behind the aluminum doors that stood between me and my eye drops, I couldn't help but wallow in my own self-pity.

This particular waiting room was white with orange chairs—the kind of plastic scoop-shaped chairs that are connected to each other by a long metal rod that holds them in line. After the noise of the dirty man incident made its way down the hall, I walked back up to the counter to inquire how much longer I would have to wait. I was, once again, told to take a seat and that I'd be called when they were ready.

Exasperated, I turned to make my way back to my seat. That's when I noticed her. She was a small woman, probably shorter than 5 feet. She was dressed in a muumuu—one of those brightly patterned house coats with a zipper from top to bottom. She had amazingly kind eyes and a calm demeanor.

She was seated at one end of the steel-and-metal chairs, and I was seated at the other. I thought I might be hallucinating, but the little muumuu lady seemed to be getting closer to me. Upon more inspection, I realized it wasn't my imagination. She was moving from chair to chair across the metal rail, gradually getting closer to me. After a few minutes, she ended up right beside me—plastic orange chair to plastic orange chair. There wasn't another soul in the waiting room, but she was sitting so close to me that if she moved any closer, she would have been in my lap.

"Hello," she said gently.

I peered at her with my sticky eyes and returned her greeting with a faint and possibly disinterested, "hello."

Without any encouragement from me, she began to share her story. "Did you see that man they just brought in? That's my husband."

She told me about their life and their son. He was the absolute light of their lives. Smart and handsome, he loved fixing cars with his dad. He was working at the local service station to make some extra money before college started. He would be the first in their family to pursue a higher education.

But their son was dead—killed a week before in a random shooting at the service station.

The woman explained that her husband couldn't manage the grief. He would struggle to find sleep and then reel into fits when he woke and recalled the reality of the situation.

The people at the hospital knew her and her husband by name. They were intimately familiar with the events and did everything they could to help care for them both. That was how they ended up there again this particular morning.

My selfish and insensitive heart transformed that morning. My view of the world and the people in it was forever altered. I felt the full weight of embarrassment and shame over my initial perception and judgement of this man, who transformed in my mind from a filthy addict to a loving father. I was lost in the pasture, and a small angel in a muumuu changed my direction and the course of my life.

We talked until the nurse called my name. I reluctantly got up from my seat and met with the doctor, who gave me the eye drops. I wanted to stay and talk to the lady, but it was time for me to go. We hugged, and I headed back to the Marriott. I swung by the gift shop and grabbed a pair of glasses. By noon, I was in my meeting.

I can't remember a thing that happened at that meeting. But I can't forget the lessons I learned that day. My career would end up taking me to amazing places and exposing me to all kinds of interesting people. Hospitality, after all, is about taking care of people. In 20 years, I've met all kinds: happy celebrating people, business travelers, prostitutes, retirees, angry people determined to let me have it over coffee that's gone cold or a stray hair on the bathroom floor, and associates with complicated lives raising families on minimum-wage earnings. Since my emergency room revelation, I can honestly say that I connect with each of them from a place of love and the absence of judgement.

Like Joseph wandering, I was quite lost. I had an interaction with a stranger who changed the course of my life. There was absolutely no Earthly reason we should have met. The course of events that brought us together can only have been fate. The impact she had on what I do as well as who I am is immeasurable. I was certain that the course of events that transpired that day in Providence would doom my career, when in fact they caused it to flourish. I could have never made it in a world of scathing YELP reviews without the life lessons and intercession of my beloved muumuu lady.

The Beliefnet website has a search for "How to tell if you've encountered an angel in human form?" It reads, "Angels who appear as humans, often have very kind eyes and a peaceful calming energy. They are remarkably helpful, and they usually don't say much though what they do say is very poignant. It is far more common for angels to appear in physical form as humans, than wearing wings."

I should reach out to them and correct their site with an update: "Sometimes their wings are tucked under their muumuus."

Hospitality and the Holy Spirit

Dear Lord, Thank you for the angels you have sent to me and the lessons I have learned from them. Please help me to not need to get pink eye or some other ailment in order to wake up and pay attention to people around me and their needs. Help me to show kindness and compassion in every situation. Amen.

Lost and Found

Parable of the Lost Son

To illustrate the point further, Jesus told them this story: "A man had two sons. The younger son told his father, 'I want my share of your estate now before you die.' So his father agreed to divide his wealth between his sons.

"A few days later this younger son packed all his belongings and moved to a distant land, and there he wasted all his money in wild living. About the time his money ran out, a great famine swept over the land, and he began to starve. He persuaded a local farmer to hire him, and the man sent him into his fields to feed the pigs. The young man became so hungry that even the pods he was feeding the pigs looked good to him. But no one gave him anything.

"When he finally came to his senses, he said to himself, 'At home even the hired servants have food enough to spare, and here I am dying of hunger! I will go home to my father and say, "Father, I have sinned against both heaven and you, and I am no longer worthy of being called your son. Please take me on as a hired servant."'

"So he returned home to his father. And while he was still a long way off, his father saw him coming. Filled with love and compassion, he ran to his son, embraced him, and kissed him. His son said to him, 'Father, I have sinned against both heaven and you, and I am no longer worthy of being called your son.'

"But his father said to the servants, 'Quick! Bring the finest

*robe in the house and put it on him. Get a ring for his finger
and sandals for his feet. And kill the calf we have been
fattening. We must celebrate with a feast, for this son of mine
was dead and has now returned to life. He was lost, but now
he is found.' So the party began.*

*"Meanwhile, the older son was in the fields working. When he
returned home, he heard music and dancing in the house, and
he asked one of the servants what was going on. 'Your brother
is back,' he was told, 'and your father has killed the fattened
calf. We are celebrating because of his safe return.'*

*"The older brother was angry and wouldn't go in. His father
came out and begged him, but he replied, 'All these years I've
slaved for you and never once refused to do a single thing
you told me to. And in all that time you never gave me even
one young goat for a feast with my friends. Yet when this
son of yours comes back after squandering your money on
prostitutes, you celebrate by killing the fattened calf!'*

*"His father said to him, 'Look, dear son, you have always
stayed by me, and everything I have is yours. We had to
celebrate this happy day. For your brother was dead and has
come back to life! He was lost, but now he is found!'*
(Luke 15:11–32 NLT)

The story of the prodigal son is perhaps the most notable lost-and-
found story of the Bible.

Parable of the Lost Sheep
*Now the tax collectors and sinners were all gathering around
to hear Jesus. But the Pharisees and the teachers of the law
muttered, "This man welcomes sinners and eats with them."
Then Jesus told them this parable: "Suppose one of you has
a hundred sheep and loses one of them. Doesn't he leave the
ninety-nine in the open country and go after the lost sheep*

until he finds it? And when he finds it, he joyfully puts it on
his shoulders and goes home. Then he calls his friends and
neighbors together and says, 'Rejoice with me; I have found
my lost sheep.' I tell you that in the same way there will be
more rejoicing in heaven over one sinner who repents than
over ninety-nine righteous persons who do not need to repent."
(Luke 15:1–7 NIV)

What does this passage inform us about the Bible's views on hospitality?
Every day guests check out and leave items behind in their rooms.

As the rhyme goes, "Dear St. Anthony, Please come around,
something is lost, and it cannot be found."

St. Anthony was a Catholic priest who became a saint famous for
his connection to lost things and the poor. If he has a passion for lost
things, St. Anthony would have had a field-day in the hotel business.

Have you ever wondered what the journey looks like for the items
that are left behind? Here's a peek into the life of a forgotten item.
On the day you check out, your room is designated as "vacant-dirty."
Vacant-dirty rooms are scheduled to be cleaned and prepared for a
new arrival, versus "occupied-dirty," which designates that the room
is a stay-over. As an industry standard, stayover rooms are cleaned
differently. Unless the guests request more frequent laundry service,
linens are changed only every three days during a guests contiguous
stay, and terrycloth towels that are hung up are intended to be left in the
room for guest use instead of changed every day.

This policy changed more than a decade ago as conservation efforts
become a priority and has had a wonderful impact. You've probably
read the card in your room that reads, "Every day, millions of gallons
of water are used to clean hotel bed linens and towels. As part of our
conservation efforts, our policy is to change linens every third day of
your stay. If you'd like your sheets changed daily, please leave this card
on your pillow, and we are happy to accommodate your request. Any
towels hung up will be left for your continued use, and we will remove

and replace those on the floor."

You get the idea: A check-out room, obviously receives a deep and thorough clean, whereas a stay-over room gets an express clean. On the day of a guest's departure, any items found in the room are collected. They are placed in a bag, typically the same type of bags that are hanging in the closet for dry cleaning services, which is labeled with the room number and date. The room attendant places the bags on the cleaning supplies cart and continues through the assigned "board" of rooms. The supervisor circulates throughout the day, checking on room status, assisting attendants, and collecting the bags of lost-and-found items. In 20 years, I don't think I've worked a single day when we haven't collected multiple tagged bags of lost-and-found items.

As an industry standard, hotels must keep lost-and-found items for 90 days. Items are logged into a database, so if someone calls about an item, we can check quickly if we have it.

In our hotel, we have 12 large bins labeled with the months of the year. The bags are placed in the appropriate monthly bin, where they stay for the next 90 days.

We don't call guests to let them know that we have their items in our lost and found. Quite frankly, that would be a full-time job for someone. The exception to this policy is high-value items. If you leave a laptop, tablet, diamond ring, or other valuable item, we'll call you to let you know.

When a guest calls to ask for an item, we check the database. If we have it, we politely ask how they'd like to pay for the cost of shipping it to them the reality is that most of these items become long-term guests of the bins.

What happens after 90 days? Good question. The first day of each month, we take that month's bin and dump it out on a table. The housekeepers are allowed to keep any items that they turned in. If they don't want an item, it remains on the table for other hotel employees to take.

Some items are kept as a small inventory of items that we know future guests may need. "You're here for a wedding but forgot to pack your black belt? Yes, sir, I may be able to assist with that." We donate the rest of the lost-and-found items to local charities.

I always get two questions in a lost-and-found conversation: What's the most common item in lost and found? What's the strangest item ever left behind in your hotel?

The most common item is chargers—by far. We have every size, shape, color, model, and style of charger you could imagine. Very few people are interested in paying to have a charger returned to them, so we end up with an impressive collection that includes a variety of international and universal chargers as well as some that I have no idea what they're for. The charger bins are an exciting place to take guests who forgot to pack their chargers and their batteries are about to die. Their eyes light up when they see the coiled cables available for their use and realize that battery life-support is on hand.

The strangest item? One day, I walked into my office, and in the middle of the floor was a prosthetic leg with a lost-and-found tag on it. I paused for a moment and looked around for the "Candid Cameras" that I expect to find in moments like this. This definitely was a high-value item requiring a call! From the tag, I had the guest's contact information so I called the now-checked-out-and-traveling guest. The call to this particular guest went something like this: "Sir, good morning. I'm glad I reached you. You checked out of our hotel this morning, and I believe you left something behind."

After a brief pause, he replied, "Oh! My leg."

Apparently, he travels with multiple legs. I confess that I posted a "just when you thought you'd seen it all" photo on my Facebook page, and then I spent the remainder of my morning trying to fit the leg into a box and ship it to the hotel where he was traveling next.

Then there was the day I found a person.

I'll never forget that day. It was late morning. The breakfast rush was over, and most of our guests were already off to work or in their meeting rooms when yelling was heard from the business center. Immediately,

Hospitality and the Holy Spirit

the front desk team investigated the shouting, and they came to get me. A woman was sitting at the computer, attempting to read something on the screen. Despite the fact that the font was huge, she was yelling that she couldn't see the messages in her e-mail.

I let the woman know I was there to help, calmed her down, and began to investigate the situation. Sadly, it became apparent that she had accompanied a gentleman (and I use that term lightly) to his room the night before. He had checked out and departed the hotel, leaving her behind. There was no doubt she was lost. Obviously bagging and binning her wasn't an option. She was a very high value item! I asked what her plan was, and she told me that she was going to ride the bus until they kicked her off, and then she was going to kill herself.

"Not today," I told her. "Let's find a different plan."

I don't even know the woman's real name. She had multiple hospital bracelets with a variety of names, but no identification. Eventually she passed out in the corner on a sofa in the lobby, and we called an ambulance for assistance. They drove away with her. The police said it was best that emergency responders were involved, and they would connect with the resources and help she needed. I hope those resources included hope, faith, friendship, and Jesus Christ.

"Dear God, please care for her. Help this prodigal daughter find her way home."

I've met lots of lost people, but they rarely sit in the lobby yelling at computer screens. Some enter my life as associates struggling to find their way. Others wear designer suits and seek satisfaction in material things or ego-driven recognition. Still others have vacant eyes and sip cocktails until they're tired enough to sleep.

I pray to St. Anthony to celebrate the rediscovery of lost things. It seems the world is full of lost sheep in need of a shepherd to guide them home. Maybe we all have moments in our lives where we're lost and need hope, faith, Jesus Christ, and the joy of celebration when we're found.

*Dear Lord, Thank you for finding me when I feel lost.
Thank you for sending your word to guide me when I find
myself tangled up at the bottom of the lost-and-found bin.
Help me to have more found moments than lost moments
and help me to help others find their way home too. Amen.*

What Do You Thirst For?

*But whosoever drinketh of the water that I shall give him shall
never thirst; but the water that I shall give him shall be in him
a well of water springing up into everlasting life.*
(John 4:14 KJV)

In John, we read that on the last day—that great day of the feast—Jesus
stood and cried, saying, "If any man thirst, let him come unto me and
drink."

I don't imagine that Jesus was saying, "Anyone who hasn't had their
coffee this morning and is suffering from a moderate addiction should
come forward, and I'll grind up some beans for you so you can have
something to drink." He is clearly referring to a thirst for salvation. The
only way to pour righteousness into the vacant belly of our soul and
satiate our deepest void is to thirst for Christ. Okay, that may sound a
bit dramatic, but many Bible verses refer to the "thirst" for Christ. One
of my favorites is John 4:14 above.

Have you seen signs professing a love of coffee? "I only need coffee
on days ending with Y." "I'll start working when my coffee does."

The world is crazy for coffee. Anyone who's spent a morning in
a hotel lobby can attest to the passion people have for a good cup of
coffee. In my experience, about half of Americans are true java junkies
and drink coffee every day. They're passionate about the stuff! If the
coffee isn't ready, hot, and available in a very large cup, you'll have to

answer to the dark side of a daily coffee drinker.

Actually, hoteliers love guests who are passionate about—and slightly addicted to—coffee. They are great for business. The coffee bar in a hotel lobby can generate $3,000 a month and contribute lots of profit to the bottom line. A gourmet coffee bar in San Francisco sells coffee for $75 per cup, and they sell out daily. Coffee is profitable, and it's inexpensive to produce. After all, it's mostly water.

Our obsession with coffee is obvious. Some people plan their entire mornings and daily rituals around acquiring and enjoying coffee. Coffee can be hot, steamed, cold, iced, or pressed, and it's used to flavor just about everything from ice cream to dental floss. If you ever question the power of coffee, just try to explain to a guest why you don't have any.

Coffee has been elevated to the status of religious ritual; however, it had a very modest origin. The story goes that goat herders in Ethiopia and Yemen noticed a behavior change in their goats after they ate coffee beans. The goats seemed livelier—maybe even happier. The goat herders did the logical thing and tried to eat the beans themselves. After some experimentation, they found the most successful approach was to grind the beans and add them to water. Voilà! Coffee!

The preparation of coffee hasn't changed all that dramatically since then. Coffee is still ground and combined with water. What has changed is the presentation and conversation surrounding it. There's a market for both Maxwell House and Starbucks. As long as it's coffee, people will pay for it. Why? Are we truly addicted to coffee?

Because coffee is a stimulant, it's categorized as "mildly addictive." I don't believe it is an addiction as much as it is something we desire and "thirst for." We've built a culture around coffee. It's trendy for teens, edgy for executives, and heavenly for hoteliers.

The only thing that sells better than coffee at our hotels is water. The prettier the bottle and more refreshing sounding the name, the better: Evian, Pure, Life, Kona, Bling. Half of Americans drink coffee every day, but all of us require water. We've elevated the water drinking experience to the point where the tap is taboo. There's no doubt we are all thirsty.

Jesus is truly the Figi water for a thirsty soul. Why are we drinking so many brightly packaged beverages? The environment and ocean animals are drowning in our discarded bottles, yet church attendance and number of believers continue to decline. We're living in a thirsty world, yet we continue to seek unsatisfying options. We consume gallons of coffee and bottled water that will never come close to quenching our thirst.

I think I'll set up an experiment. On one side of the hotel lobby, I'll serve hot, overpriced cups of coffee guaranteed to leave you thirsty. On the other side, I'll set up communion: a thimble full of wine representing the blood of Jesus Christ and guaranteed to quench your thirst for as long as you live and beyond. I wonder what the morning rush would look like. Where would the lines form?

Maybe the most attractive answer isn't an "either or" decision. Maybe it's an "and" decision. If you choose Jesus, you don't have to give up coffee. You can have both! The real questions are: What do you truly "thirst" for? Which line would you go to first?

Dear Lord, Please help me to step away
from empty calories. Sometimes I eat and drink things that sit
on the surface of my body as fat without nourishing me.
Help me to make better choices and consume things that satisfy
and nourish—well that and maybe just a couple
of M&Ms too, just for sweetness. Thank you for your word
and the need it fills. Amen.

500 Pounds of Turkey
and 100 Cases of Coca-Cola

Meanwhile, the apostles gathered around Jesus and brought Him news of all they had done and taught. And He said to them, "Come with Me privately to a solitary place, and let us rest for a while." For many people were coming and going, and they did not even have time to eat.

So they went away in a boat by themselves to a solitary place. But many people saw them leaving and recognized them. They ran together on foot from all the towns and arrived before them. When Jesus stepped ashore and saw a large crowd, He had compassion on them, because they were like sheep without a shepherd. And He began to teach them many things.

By now the hour was already late. So the disciples came to Jesus and said, "This is a desolate place, and the hour is already late. Dismiss the crowd so they can go to the surrounding countryside and villages and buy themselves something to eat."

But Jesus told them, "You give them something to eat."

They asked Him, "Should we go out and spend two hundred denariif to give all of them bread to eat?"

"Go and see how many loaves you have," He told them.

And after checking, they said, "Five—and two fish."

Then Jesus directed them to have the people sit in groups on the green grass. So they sat down in groups of hundreds and fifties.

Taking the five loaves and the two fish and looking up to
heaven, Jesus spoke a blessing and broke the loaves. Then He
gave them to His disciples to set before the people. And He
divided the two fish among them all.
They all ate and were satisfied, and the disciples picked up
twelve basketfuls of broken pieces of bread and fish. And there
were five thousand men who had eaten the loaves.
(Mark 6:30–44 BSB)

This story is the epitome of hospitality—providing plenty in the midst
of scarcity.

This is one of my favorite Bible stories. I can close my eyes and
clearly see the convening crowd of 5,000 people pursuing Jesus and
gathering on a grassy hill with hopes of hearing him speak and being
healed, inspired, and enlightened to the possibilities of God almighty,
the Messiah, and an eternal life in heaven. I can see the slightly soiled
face of a dark-haired boy wearing a neutral colored tunic, with a red
belt and worn leather sandals (what can I say, my imagination works in
color and high definition), carrying five pita-size loaves of bread and
two sardines in a sack prepared for him to provide a small lunch.

Although I don't read of it anywhere in the Bible, the mom in me
imagines his mother preparing the sack of food and making sure he
didn't forget it when he left the house that morning. I can only imagine
that she didn't have any idea what would happen that afternoon, how
significant that tidy sack of lunch would be and how her son's generosity
would be the catalyst for an amazing miracle recounted in each Gospel
book of the Bible.

Today, we worry about our kids sharing their lunches. Have nuts
been anywhere near their organically packaged, sugar-free, animal-
shaped fruit snacks? Heaven forbid they eat from the wrong side of
the food pyramid or try something that we haven't preapproved as
acceptable for both nourishment and presentation.

Thank God, this young boy's mama raised him differently. He was among the crowd that day with the heart of a servant. When asked, he offered his lunch, which by all means would have seemed insufficient and insignificant.

That's the kind of heart I hope to cultivate within my chest—the kind that offers whatever I have, even though my mind would try to convince me that it's not nearly enough to share, so I might as well go ahead and eat it myself. We all know the story. Jesus blessed the bread and the fish and asked the disciples to distribute the food to the crowd. The absolute miracle is that there was more than enough to feed all 5,000 people—not just for them to take a bite, but for them to eat as much as they wanted. A miracle!

It gets even better, and more significant, as we understand Jesus' next request for the disciple. "Gather the pieces that are left over. Let nothing be wasted." (John 6:13) They gathered the leftovers and filled 12 baskets with what was left over.

What I love about this story is the shift from scarcity to abundance. As clearly as I can picture this scene playing out in my imaginative mind, I've seen it happen in real life!

In the hospitality business, we feed people. Millions of dollars of our budget each year is generated through banquets and functions that are planned to the finest detail. Crudité platters, well-seasoned entrées, petite desserts, and gluten-free options are all planned in advance, ordered from the freshest vendors, prepared by experts with culinary pedigrees that read like the Who's Who of great chefs, and served by white glove–covered hands attached to bow-tie wearing servers. The idea of spontaneously feeding 5,000 people strikes a fear in my heart that only those who understand this process could relate to.

Luckily a braver soul, named Kostas, understood the type of abundance described in John chapter 6. About 20 years before I began writing this story, Kostas put the wheels in motion of one of the greatest examples of hospitality that I've ever witnessed. The holidays in the hotel business are truly the best time of the year. We specialize in gatherings and celebrations; that's where we really get to shine. From the moment the glittering décor springs to life in our ballrooms and lobbies around Thanksgiving, to the midnight toast on New Year's Eve, hospitality is running through our veins like the free pour of a perfect peppermint martini. That's with the exception of one day: Christmas eve.

On that day, everything in the hotel comes to a screeching halt. That's when everyone gathers with loved ones in their homes. Our hotel lights continue to twinkle. However, occupancy drops, and the ballrooms are vacant.

Kostas saw an opportunity. He had a heart that recognized there were neighbors in our cities who wouldn't be gathering in homes with mistletoe, eggnog, hot food, colorfully wrapped presents, and antics from eccentric relatives. Kostas wanted to fill the ballroom on Christmas eve, not because we needed more revenue per square foot, but because there were families in our hometown who wouldn't have an abundant Christmas, children who wouldn't be opening presents, and people who were homeless and cold.

Kostas began to make calls. One local business offered their "sack of fishes and loaves." The Jaindl family, a local farm, provided turkeys, and they came to serve it themselves. Laneco, a local grocery store, delivered truckloads of food. Our local Coca-Cola bottler dropped off more than 100 cases of beverages. Toys for Tots gave us everything that was in their storage facilities. Local bus-line Trans Bridge ran their luxury busses throughout the day to pick up the folks and families who had nowhere to go and nothing else for Christmas.

We served more than 5,000 people that day. Have you ever seen 5,000 people eating? If so, you can truly understand the miracle of the loaves and fishes. I have, and it's amazing.

God shined down on this event. The Holy Spirit was at work in each of us as we watched our fears that there wouldn't be enough subside into baskets of leftovers.

That was 20 years ago, and we've held this event every Christmas eve since. I still find myself panicking, worrying there might not be enough food, gifts, and cheer to go around. When will I learn that I'm not in charge—even when I think I am? What more will it take for me to realize the abundance of the Lord and the generosity of our community? Why do I sometimes still think I should "just eat my small sack of lunch, since it won't be enough to make a difference anyway?"

Each year, our local Cops 'n Kids program, founded by Beverly Bradley, brings books to our event. Their SUV-sleigh arrives with stacks of books and a gaggle of volunteers who make certain that after everyone has eaten "as much as they wanted," and every child has gifts from Santa, they also leave with a brand-new book.

I believe there are angels among us. One year, in a moment of weakness, when the entire event seemed too much to manage and the world seemed too commercial—even unmanageable and ungrateful—Beverly whispered to me, "If things seem chaotic, look down."

What she meant was, look down past the whirling typhoon of wrappings and garbage, past the mountain of dirty dishes, and past the noise of shouting over the Christmas carols, and focus on the faces of the children. I did look down, and I clearly recall seeing the slightly soiled face of the dark-haired boy in the tunic with the red belt. Well, okay, he wasn't actually wearing a tunic, and I'm pretty sure it was chocolate on his smiling face not dirt, but he did have dark hair, and he was wearing a red belt.

That young boy handed me a gift. It was a red envelope with a card inside. Two snowmen were pictured on the cover that read, "Merry Christmas." The message inside said, "Wishing you a Merry Christmas." The hand-written signature said, "Thank you – God Bless Marazzani / Rivera family." My favorite part was a drawing of a heart made with a purple crayon. I keep that card in my desk as a reminder to "share my lunch."

I encourage you to share yours as well. Perhaps the solution to the scarcity in the world can be found in this Bible lesson, giving what we have, even when it seems insignificant, allowing God to bless it while we watch in amazement what's possible.

This Christmas eve, I'll take Beverly's advice and look down. More importantly, I'll also look up and give thanks to God for what I have, the desire to share it, and the reminder that true hospitality isn't about what we earn, but what we're willing to share.

Dear Lord, Please keep me from viewing the world as scarce. Help me to see the abundance in your creation and my life and to share it willingly. Help me to be grateful and generous. Amen.

Preparing for His Arrival

"But about that day or hour no one knows, not even the angels in heaven, nor the Son, but only the Father. As it was in the days of Noah, so it will be at the coming of the Son of Man. For in the days before the flood, people were eating and drinking, marrying and giving in marriage, up to the day Noah entered the ark; and they knew nothing about what would happen until the flood came and took them all away. That is how it will be at the coming of the Son of Man. Two men will be in the field; one will be taken and the other left. Two women will be grinding with a hand mill; one will be taken and the other left.

"Therefore keep watch, because you do not know on what day your Lord will come. But understand this: If the owner of the house had known at what time of night the thief was coming, he would have kept watch and would not have let his house be broken into. So you also must be ready, because the Son of Man will come at an hour when you do not expect him.

"Who then is the faithful and wise servant, whom the master has put in charge of the servants in his household to give them their food at the proper time? It will be good for that servant whose master finds him doing so when he returns. Truly I tell you, he will put him in charge of all his possessions. But suppose that servant is wicked and says to himself, 'My master is staying away a long time,' and he then begins to beat his

*fellow servants and to eat and drink with drunkards. The
master of that servant will come on a day when he does not
expect him and at an hour he is not aware of. He will cut him
to pieces and assign him a place with the hypocrites, where
there will be weeping and gnashing of teeth"*
(Matthew 24:36–51 NIV)

When you open a new hotel, there's always some fluctuation to the opening date. I've never been involved in a project where we set an opening date and actually checked guests in on that day. It takes over a year to build a hotel. If you think about everything that happens in construction and then consider the initial set up of each guest room as well as hiring and training every staff member, it's pretty obvious why the opening date is a moving target.

Before you can take reservations and get some actual business on the books, the process includes a number of benchmarks. If your opening date is set for April 5th, the reservations system may initially begin accepting reservations for some time in October. As you hit specific criteria and benchmarks in your progress, the date you're available and accepting reservations will shift closer and close the gap of time between the target opening date and the date a potential guest can make a reservation. These two dates gradually dance toward each other until you're in the final stages of preparation and looking at your system to prepare for arriving guests.

I'll always remember the anticipation for an opening that was scheduled for April 5th. We were on pace and ready to open our doors on April 9th. Due to the reservations availability dance, you could only make reservations for the night of April 9th for three days. We had one reservation for the night we were opening: Mr. Bouffard.

Every associate and manager built their entire day around the anticipated arrival of Mr. Bouffard. Every shift stood at attention, eagerly anticipating his graceful steps through our spotless front door and across the polished yellow tile to the sparkling granite and marble front desk. Every uniform was perfect, every nametag was straight, and every heart was beating with anticipation of practicing our new skills. You could still smell fresh paint and Ecolab all-purpose cleaner as we stood at attention and waited for his arrival.

Hours passed, shifts changed, and our spines began to slump as our postures slipped from full attention to a more relaxed position. By 11:00 pm, there still was no Mr. Bouffard. He was a no-show. That's what we call someone who has a confirmed reservation, however, for whatever reason they never make an appearance and neglect to cancel their reservation so they are charged for the stay without ever allowing us to impress and amaze them with our fresh faces and newly laundered sheets.

That was more than 11 years ago. I still wonder what happened to the mysterious Mr. Bouffard that night. We didn't have any reservations for the next night so we filled our time with additional training and polishing of silverware, which really didn't need it considering it hadn't been used since we removed it from its packaging and polished it less than 48 hours before.

Our nametags were lazily piled in the center of the table, and we passed the time with casual conversation and taking selfies.

Imagine our surprise when a guest burst through the door, dragging wheeled luggage behind him. We jumped to attention and grabbed any nametag within reach in an effort to create the impression that we were ready for this new arriving guest. He was a walk-in—a guest without a reservation who walks into the hotel and requests a room for the night.

This particular guest was driving by, saw our illuminated sign, and decided to see if he could get a room. Of course, he could! We had more than 150 available rooms and a full team of associates who wanted to check him in, bring him extra towels, prepare his breakfast, offer him lunch and dinner and a cocktail, personally program his wake-up call, and drive him around in the shuttle. We would have also read him a bedtime story and tucked him in if he'd have let us.

The guest on April 10th came and went, and thousands of guests

Hospitality and the Holy Spirit

have followed since then. Every morning we prepare for our arrivals, research their preferences, review their prior stays at our property and also other properties in our brand, add their favorite beverages to their in-room refrigerators, carefully place allergy free pillows in their rooms, draft hand-written welcome notes, and place welcome amenities in clean and inspected rooms that anxiously anticipate an overnight companion.

I learned my lessons from the Mr. Bouffard slip: Never again get distracted and caught off-guard by a walk-in guest. Always keep eyes on the door in anticipation of the next opportunity to offer assistance to a guest waltzing through the porte cochere and gliding between automated glass doors.

We review arrival reports every day. We prepare and anticipate. We make sure that everything and everyone is in their places for the best possible first impression and to set the stage for a great guest experience.

We want our guests to feel like we have nothing more important to do than study their reservations, customize their suites, and await their arrivals. This is much more challenging with a walk-in guest, who arrives without a confirmed reservation. That's when our genuine desire to serve and hospitality spirit must take over and guide the unscripted interactions and spur-of-the-moment room assignments that must take place.

It's a joy to watch a seasoned service associate serve a walk-in. This is terrifying for a new associate who now needs to manage an engaging conversation as they navigate the technology to assign a room, create an electronic key, confirm payment and identification, and somehow make this guest feel as welcome as the other 100 arrivals on their shift.

In the Bible, Matthew tells us of Jesus' return. Guess what? He doesn't have a reservation.

One thing is for certain. Much like the floating dates on the calendar that represent the space from a hotel target opening date to the reservation availability date, the gap between the ascension of the Lord and His return gets smaller with every passing day.

"But of that day and hour no one knows, not even the angels of heaven, but My Father only. But as the days of Noah were, so also will the coming of the Son of Man be. For as in the days before the flood, they were eating and drinking, marrying and giving in marriage, until the day that Noah entered the ark, and did not know until the flood came and took them all away, so also will the coming of the Son of Man be. Then two men will be in the field: one will be taken and the other left. Two women will be grinding at the mill: one will be taken and the other left. Watch therefore, for you do not know what hour your Lord is coming. But know this, that if the master of the house had known what hour the thief would come, he would have watched and not allowed his house to be broken into. Therefore you also be ready, for the Son of Man is coming at an hour you do not expect." (Matthew 24:36–44 NIV)

I read these words and feel my tummy flutter like a new associate worrying about the unexpected arrival of an important guest. Unlike Mr. Bouffard, who at the very worst could shame me on Trip Advisor for a poor arrival experience and grant me a poor score on a Marriott guest survey, the stakes are much higher with the return of Christ. I can only imagine the chaos as we attempt to reach into a huge pile of discarded nametags and rush to create the impression that we are prepared and ready. We won't be able to fake it.

The one thing I've learned is that the more I practice for an unexpected guest's arrival, the more comfortable I am when it happens. I can actually move along the spectrum from fear to anticipation with every role play and every opportunity to practice the conversations and keystrokes that make for a great arrival experience.

Maybe I can also practice for the biggest arrival the world will ever know. I can practice the behaviors and intentions that will be revealed at that moment. I can make sure my nametag isn't in a dusty pile of regrets, but rather pinned squarely on my chest, reflecting a life of anticipation, service, and hospitality.

Dear Lord, Help me to be ready—ready to act when opportunities to serve and share present themselves. Please send the holy spirit to snap me out of it if I get distracted and help me make progress each day on the journey to be my best self. Amen.

Blessed Is He

The Beatitudes
Looking up at His disciples, Jesus said:
"Blessed are you who are poor,
for yours is the kingdom of God.
Blessed are you who hunger now,
for you will be filled.
Blessed are you who weep now,
for you will laugh.
Blessed are you when people hate you, and when they exclude
you and insult you and reject your name as evil because of the
Son of Man. Rejoice in that day and leap for joy, because great
is your reward in heaven. For their fathers treated the prophets
in the same way. (Luke 6:20–23 BSB)

Woes to the Satisfied
But woe to you who are rich,
for you have already received your comfort.
Woe to you who are well fed now,
for you will hunger.
Woe to you who laugh now,
for you will mourn and weep.
Woe to you when all men speak well of you,
for their fathers treated the false prophets in the same way
(Luke 6:24–26 BSB)

Hospitality and the Holy Spirit

I approached writing this book with the goal of learning about the Bible. I wanted to find a systematic way to study the messages of the Bible with the intention of using them as a filter through which I could evaluate my life and hopefully discover that, as a Christian, I am doing okay.

I absolutely believe Jesus died for my sins and that through his grace—and only through his grace—I will find eternal life. If I'm being completely honest, however, there are parts of the Bible that scare me. One example is the Beatitudes. The sayings are rhythmic and lovely. It's the warning that follows that makes me so uncomfortable.

Even if I could wrap my brain around the impact of these sentences delivered by Jesus in the Sermon on the Mount and somehow manage to convince myself that I'm not on the wrong side of the equation, it's impossible to argue the clarity of Matthew's supporting argument. "Again I tell you, it is easier for a camel to go through the eye of a needle than for someone who is rich to enter the kingdom of God." (Matthew 19:24)

Don't get me wrong. I'm not the type most would consider rich, but I must admit that I have never known what it means to be poor. The closest I've come to understanding hunger is on a day when I happen to miss both breakfast and lunch. On the surface, it's easy to recognize that I'm at risk.

I've been carrying around a bulletin from a church service that took place more than a month ago. The sermon on that Sunday was about interpreting the Beatitudes. Reverend McGowan's message that morning helped to redirect my anxiety to a less literal interpretation of this passage. He introduced the concept of a hunger for Christ and a conscious effort not to fill our lives with clutter that limits the space we have to receive the Holy Spirit and allow him to live and work within us.

Ok, maybe I just need to take a deep breath and step around the landmines that can shift my soul from the "blessed are" category to the "woe to you" category.

So, what does this have to do with hospitality? I live and work in a world where "no vacancy" equals "success." In the hotel business, it's easy to adopt a "heads in beds" mentality that celebrates "full." This is the same world where Priceline and Expedia are mass marketing to the public. Hotels have empty rooms that need to be filled, and you can buy them online and get an amazing deal. The truth, however, is that great hospitality isn't about running at 100 percent occupancy. As a matter of fact, there are actually times when it is in your best interest not to sell 100 percent of your inventory.

I'd like to share two concepts as I attempt to explain "blessed" and "no vacancy" from a hospitality perspective. The first is perishability, and the second is REVPAR.

"Perishable" means that something has a shelf life. It doesn't last forever. If it isn't consumed in a certain period of time, it's rotten and worthless. Food is perishable. Most food has a shelf life of less than seven days. Even if it's properly stored, it really shouldn't be eaten after one week's time.

A hotel room is also perishable. For the sake of simple math, think of it like this. A 100-room hotel has 365 days per year to sell 100 rooms each night; it actually has 36,500 room nights as opposed to 100 rooms. A room not sold on a particular night will sit empty, and after 24 hours it can no longer be sold on that night. It's worthless and a missed opportunity. Once we understand perishability, the urgency around occupancy seems to make sense.

That's where REVPAR—revenue per available room—comes into play. The fun part of hotel operations is that every day, every 24 hours, is a pure exercise in economics 101 and the lesson of supply and demand. We constantly balance demand (occupancy) with supply (daily rate) to generate the best possible financial return. We evaluate our success by REVPAR. This is how we can compare the results of a 100-room hotel to a 500-room hotel and determine which hotel is doing a better job of managing both occupancy and average daily rate. If I decided to charge a $10 rate, I could run at 100 percent occupancy every day. But our staff and property would be exhausted and, the nightly revenue wouldn't

Hospitality and the Holy Spirit

even come close to covering the expenses. The key is to recognize the urgency of perishability and manage market demand to deliver the best possible revenue per available room. Long-term hotel success comes from a REVPAR focus, not a "heads in beds, fill every room every night" approach. Perhaps my life as a Christian is the same.

I sometimes catch myself at the end of the day amazed at the race I've run, falsely impressed by my stamina and the checkmarks on my completed to-do list. Then I remember that I need to think about my personal REVPAR and the Beatitudes. I need to consciously hunger and make space for Christ and the Holy Spirit. I need to hang a "do not disturb" sign on a spacious suite located in my heart to protect myself from the false sense of accomplishment that comes with a cluttered life and the inability to walk away from unnecessary fillers that do nothing to advance my greater purpose.

I've spent time thinking about my purpose and the why behind what I do. My personal intention is to live a life that demonstrates hospitality and kindness. There's no way I can fit a camel through the eye of a needle, and it's a daily struggle to embrace the thought of "vacant" moments where I can make space for prayer and purpose.

I do like the idea of the Beatitudes. I like small statements that generate big thoughts. Here are some modern day-hospitality themed stay-attitudes that could improve our travel behaviors and would certainly be pleasing to hotel associates.

- Blessed is he who checks out by noon
for theirs is the room that can be ready for a guest arriving at 3pm.
- Blessed is he who doesn't steal the towels
for his is the credit card that will not be charged for missing items.
- Blessed is he who takes only what he can eat from the buffet
for his clean plate will not generate unnecessary waste of food.
- Blessed is he who wears pajamas
for he will not have to fear sleepwalking and losing his room key.

Dear Lord, Help me to continue to make space in my life for you and your word. Help me to seek something better than being busy. You and I both know how much I like to be busy. Help me get off of the hamster wheel and walk calmly and confidently to a stronger purpose today. Amen.

Who Do You Serve?
Servant-Leadership and the Last Supper

*"It was just before the Passover Festival. Jesus knew that
the hour had come for him to leave this world and go to the
Father. Having loved his own who were in the world, he loved
them to the end.*

*The evening meal was in progress, and the devil had already
prompted Judas, the son of Simon Iscariot, to betray Jesus.
Jesus knew that the Father had put all things under his power,
and that he had come from God and was returning to God;
so he got up from the meal, took off his outer clothing, and
wrapped a towel around his waist. After that, he poured water
into a basin and began to wash his disciples' feet, drying them
with the towel that was wrapped around him."*

(John 13:1–5 NIV)

This is a remarkable part of the Last Supper story. The host, Jesus, gets
up from the dinner table, removes the guests' shoes, and begins to wash
their feet. Could you imagine being a guest at a meal where someone
removed your shoes and washed your feet?

This isn't the first time that we read of this gesture from Jesus in the
Bible. It's easy to dismiss it as something that we just don't do anymore,
but where this gesture becomes truly remarkable is when we understand
that Jesus is washing the feet of the man who he knows will betray him.

The story continues in verses 12 to 17.

When he had finished washing their feet, he put on his
clothes and returned to his place. "Do you understand what
I have done for you?" he asked them. "You call me 'Teacher'
and 'Lord,' and rightly so, for that is what I am. Now that I,
your Lord and Teacher, have washed your feet, you also should
wash one another's feet. I have set you an example that you
should do as I have done for you. Very truly I tell you, no
servant is greater than his master, nor is a messenger greater
than the one who sent him. Now that you know these things,
you will be blessed if you do them. (John 13:12–17 NIV)

In an intentional act of pure service, Jesus washes the feet of all the disciples. He models generous behavior and then declares the expectation that they will treat each other with the same care and selflessness that he demonstrated to them.

Servant leadership is a popular theme of many best-selling books and seminars. If we want to measure our effectiveness as leaders, we should ask ourselves if we're willing to wash the feet of the people we serve. If you answer yes to this question, consider if you're willing to serve someone who will betray you.

In my servant's mind, I view everyone around me as my customer, and it's my responsibility to serve them. Obviously it's easy to think of the guest as my customer; however, the hotel associates, the hotel owners, the students in my hospitality 101 class, and my friends and neighbors are also my customers. I'm in the customer service industry, and I enjoy serving a variety of customers.

The truth is, I'm happy to "wash feet," and I spend quite a bit of time anticipating the needs of others and quite a bit of effort taking action to meet and exceed their needs.

I like to consider myself a servant-leader, but the truth is that I fall short. When? I fall short when it comes to Jesus' example and his selfless generosity to the one who would betray him. It's easy for me to serve people I like, those who work hard and look beautiful in pressed uniforms and polished shoes. But I'm not a true servant to anyone who I believe might betray me.

Thank goodness I'm not being kissed on the cheek and sentenced to death. The betrayals I might experience in my life are insignificant in the big picture. An associate might quit or stop showing up for work, someone might make an unflattering comment about me behind my back, or if it's really bad, they might make a scene or hurt my feelings.

Jesus knew his purpose and let nothing keep Him from living a "love thy neighbor" life. I aspire to demonstrate hospitality. I embrace the responsibility to demonstrate hospitality in all of my behaviors. That means washing the feet of everyone I serve, even those who might betray me.

It might sound easy, but it's very hard. On occasion, I've been able to give myself the necessary pep-talk and put in the extra effort to serve all of my customers, even those who represent a challenge to my kindness.

There's a young lady who works at one of our hotels. She's miserable and, dare I say, lazy. Every day for a month, I went out of my way to see her and say "Good morning" with what I hoped looked like my best smile. Each attempt was met with an eye-roll and grunt. Finally, I had it. I saw her sitting on the floor. She never seemed to stand upright; she was always sitting or leaning.

Even at stand-up meeting, she would sit or lean. You might be wondering, *what's a stand-up meeting?* Our daily stand-up meeting is when we gather before a shift and plan for the day. We discuss our arrivals, VIPs, surprise special amenities, special preparations, which guests are expected to depart that day, any functions taking place, our financials, guest reviews, and more. It's a quick 15-minute meeting, during which we all stand together and prepare for the shift. It's called stand-up because we all stand, so when someone sits during stand-up, it's obvious.

One day, I saw the associate sitting at stand-up, and I had reached the limit of my patience. I decided to confront her about it. I wasn't exactly thinking about servant leadership or Jesus when I confronted her. I was tired of forcing smiles, and I was considering writing her up, or worse.

I knew I was intimidating to this young lady, and I certainly didn't remove her shoes and offer to wash her feet. I should have.

What she shared with me was that her shoes were way too small and standing was extremely painful. Literally. Her feet were in pain.

That night, I purchased a pair of shoes, guessing the size and rounding up. I happened to bump into one of our managers when I was at the store, and I asked her to give the shoes to the grumpy associate.

Two days later, as I entered the hotel, I passed by little miss grumpy. She was wearing her new shoes—and a huge smile.

Sometimes, I know Jesus is speaking to me and teaching me lessons that are as clear as day. He removed the shoes of his disciples and showed them how he wanted them to treat each other. One of the best leadership lessons I've learned is to remove the shoes of someone I thought would "betray me" and find the sole of someone who was being pinched—someone who could, and would, serve once her feet were freed.

I've learned that leadership is about removing obstacles for others and helping them be successful. Sometimes unleashing the soul is as easy as freeing a sore sole.

Love thy customer and remember that everyone is your customer.

Dear Lord, Thank you for this lesson, for the challenges, responsibilities, and opportunities to serve and learn that come with being a leader. Amen.

Let He Who Is Without Sin
Post the First Negative Comment

"but Jesus went to the Mount of Olives.
At dawn he appeared again in the temple courts, where all the
people gathered around him, and he sat down to teach them.
The teachers of the law and the Pharisees brought in a woman
caught in adultery. They made her stand before the group
and said to Jesus, "Teacher, this woman was caught in the act
of adultery. In the Law Moses commanded us to stone such
women. Now what do you say?" They were using this question
as a trap, in order to have a basis for accusing him.
But Jesus bent down and started to write on the ground with
his finger. When they kept on questioning him, he straightened
up and said to them, "Let any one of you who is without sin be
the first to throw a stone at her." Again he stooped down and
wrote on the ground.
At this, those who heard began to go away one at a time, the
older ones first, until only Jesus was left, with the woman still
standing there. Jesus straightened up and asked her, "Woman,
where are they? Has no one condemned you?"
"No one, sir," she said.
"Then neither do I condemn you," Jesus declared. "Go now and
leave your life of sin." (John 8:1–11 NIV)

In John 8, we hear the story of Jesus' encounter with a crowd determined
to pass judgement and stone a woman to death.

Jesus had a wonderful way of seeing the people he encountered. He didn't see them as prostitutes, beggars, or diseased outcast. He looked past external observations and popular opinion to see the very best in each person. He managed to point out the faults in the mindset of the observer instead of the imperfections of the observed.

I love the lessons of the story in John because I can use them to remind myself not to follow the crowd, not to pass judgement, but to look in the mirror and be self-aware of my own imperfections before I focus on those of anyone else. As a result, I've developed a wonderful habit.

Whenever I meet someone—a student, guest, associate, the person in front of me in grocery store line—the first thing I do is discover something I like about them. It may be a physical trait, it may be a mannerism, it may be something they say, or it may be the way they interact with someone else. Sometimes it takes a few minutes to find something, but with practice, I'm always able to discover a likeable quality. Once I discover that special something that I like about someone, I take a moment to give it my full focus and attention. The more I focus on it, the bigger it becomes, and before I know it, my thoughts and perceptions are dominated by what I like about the person.

I've had both bosses and associates who have helped me practice and develop this skill: from the controlling boss who was always red in the face with anger, but was absolutely placed in my life to help me learn lessons about the type of leader I would not want to become, to the troubled associate who constantly made poor decisions in her personal relationships. This particular associate asked to meet with me one day. She was distraught, and as a consequence of another poor decision, thought she was pregnant—even worse, she thought the baby might be the result of an encounter with another associate. This conversation promised to be the foundation of a human resource nightmare. After a busy breakfast, I asked her to meet me in my office so we could discuss her situation.

A security camera in the lobby captures all of the activity at the front desk. That camera feeds into a monitor that sits atop a cabinet in my office. I can see everything happening in the lobby at any time. I was expecting her, so I watched the monitor to see when she was approaching as I mentally reviewed my list of advice I was about to thrust upon her.

As the associate came across the lobby, she stopped and bent down. There was a piece of garbage on the floor. She stopped to pick it up and discard it in the trash on her way to my office. There it was! She had made a good decision. Without being asked, she demonstrated a desire to do the right thing. She was engaged in her work and, selflessly and despite her conflict, she picked up the garbage.

I fell in love with what I had seen and what it revealed about her. I was in the "front of the house" all morning with our busy breakfast service. I had probably walked by that very piece of rubbish, but she didn't.

I was about to cast stones and realized that instead of watching the security monitor, I should be glancing in the mirror. We ended up having an enlightening conversation. The associate opened up and shared details of her upbringing and desires for her future that exposed a beauty not obvious to most.

Sometimes, I still find myself gathering up stones. Then I think of that associate and gently discard the stones in my intentional pursuit of what I like about people.

We've become a culture of critics. We post thoughtless and hurtful comments without pause and consideration. We love to point out every fault and declare it publicly with the intention of gathering a crowd to launch stones with us.

Instead of passing judgement, Jesus caused the crowd to reflect and disperse. He said to the woman "neither do I condemn you." That is the person I choose to be. Neither could I condemn you. How could I when there is something about you that I like so much.

Please don't misinterpret this behavior and my intention. On many occasions in my work, I need to have difficult conversations with associates—or even fire them. There are consequences to poor decisions and inappropriate behavior.

Those conversations used to be painful for both of us, me as the leader and the associate sitting in front of me. Since I have adopted my "find something good about every person from the minute you meet them" philosophy, the practice of coaching conversations and employment termination has completely evolved into something like this:

I do not condemn you, and I really like you, which is why I am having this important conversation or making this decision. I know that I have actually helped careers by terminating associates who weren't thriving in our environment. My heart fills with joy when I hear from associates who have left our employ only to discover their true calling and flourish.

It's so easy to find fault with someone, to think about what you don't like about a person you meet, such as a bump in their nose, a poor fashion choice, or an annoying habit. These traits, if left unchecked, become negative caricatures of the people around us. It takes discipline to retrain your thinking and seek a unique perspective. Life is better when you focus on the things you like.

Dear Lord, Please bless everyone, in this place at this time,
doing the best they can with what they have.
Help me to find something I like in everyone I meet
and let my hands be empty when stones are being gathered.
Amen.

Hospitality and the Holy Spirit

The 15-5 Rule

"When a stranger sojourns with you in your land, you shall not do him wrong. You shall treat the stranger who sojourns with you as the native among you, and you shall love him as yourself, for you were strangers in the land of Egypt: I am the Lord your God.
"You shall do no wrong in judgment, in measures of length or weight or quantity. You shall have just balances, just weights, a just ephah, and a just hin: I am the Lord your God, who brought you out of the land of Egypt. And you shall observe all my statutes and all my rules, and do them: I am the Lord."
(Leviticus 19:33-37 ESV)

This simple Bible passage reminds us of the most basic—but most important—principle in hospitality.

We call it the 15-5 rule. It's a very basic hospitality behavior—one of the first things we demonstrate for a new associate.

The 15-5 rule is simply this.

• You must make eye contact and demonstrate welcoming body language, such as open arms, good posture, and a smile, to anyone who comes within 15 feet of you.

• You must initiate a greeting, such as "good morning" or "good evening" once they are within 5 feet of you.

Sounds easy, right? Yes, but this simple behavior can change your life.

Whenever I speak with groups about hospitality, this concept is the thing they are most interested in.

New associates easily grasp the behavior behind the 15-5 rule; however, the challenge is actually putting it into practice. We literally make an X on the floor with colored tape. Using a tape measure, we measure 5 feet and place a mark. Then we measure 15 feet and place another mark.

Take a good look at the marks, the first step is to understand the perspective and the distance. How far is 15 feet? How close is 5 feet?

Now it's time to practice. First I will role model for a new associate. I stand at the X and ask them to enter the lobby as a guest. When they approach the 15-foot mark, I smile, acknowledge them, and demonstrate welcoming body language. When they reach the 5-foot tape mark, a greeting flows effortlessly from my lips. All is well.

Ok, now it's their turn. Ten times out of ten, they execute the behavior perfectly. We celebrate their achievement! We practice again, and again and I proclaim their expertise in demonstrating the 15-5 rule. At times, I conduct a little ceremony declaring that they are now experts in the 15-5 rule and the training continues.

But, in short order, something happens that erases this learning from their memory. As additional skills and behaviors are introduced, we become distracted. When guests actually fill our lobbies, restaurants, and event centers, we fall into the comfortable behavior of looking down. We focus on what is inches from us, versus observing and acknowledging what is up to 15 feet from us.

Life is like this too. It's distracting. We seek comfort and find it by focusing on what is immediately in front of us. We spend way too much time looking down, instead of looking up. Technology isn't helping. Instead of strolling through life with eyes lifted, we are scrolling through phone screens with a false sense that we are connecting to each other. I try not to generalize by generation, but I can share from experience that our younger associates sometimes find it painful to part with their virtual stimulus, actually interact face-to-face, and initiate a genuine greeting.

Hospitality and the Holy Spirit

I believe life is about the journey and even more so the people we meet along the way. Imagine what we are missing by not practicing this behavior. The 15-5 rule is a hospitality basic, but it should also be a life basic.

I've been in the industry a long time, and at the risk of sounding boastful, I'm a 15-5 beast! I can't help myself. If you dare to pass within 15 feet of me, you're going to get a warm acknowledging glance, my best smile, and some very deliberate body language—whether you want to or not. If you come within 5 feet, I will greet you with as much enthusiasm as a stewardess at the end of a long flight.

There's a consequence to my training, practice, and dedication to the 15-5 rule. Everywhere I go, people think I work there. I'm constantly asked for prices in the grocery store, directions to the closest restroom, and assistance with anything from reaching a high shelf to my opinion on a blouse in the dressing room. I attract conversation and often learn all kinds of interesting facts about people. To me, this is where the business and the practice of hospitality intersect. My mission is to share the 15-5 rule with every group and individual I speak to or coach. I have them practice it and certify as many 15-5 experts as possible. This is my answer to the question of "how can we make the world a better place?"

If you're thinking, *I could never do that. I wouldn't know what to say and initiating a greeting with a perfect stranger seems scarier than skydiving,* let me give you a couple of quick greeting tips.

• Remember that the goal is to initiate a greeting, not to receive one. You're only responsible for your own behavior. If you say "good morning" you've successfully fulfilled your 15-5 responsibility. It doesn't matter if the receiving party responds. I've had people come back to me in complete frustration that they have been practicing the 5-foot greeting. They smile, tilt their head in warm acknowledgement, and offer a glorious greeting, then nothing! No greeting in return and they think, *That's it! I'm never doing that again! I felt totally stupid.* My coaching, at that point, is to let go of the expectation, know deep inside that you're living with eyes up, awake and aware, genuinely intent to share hospitality with those around you. Pick your head up and get back into the game. This is what makes life worth living. Be brave, own your intention, and I'm certain, even if a response wasn't returned, many people will be pleasantly surprised that you noticed them and even delighted that you spoke with them.

• One word of caution. It's easiest to practice this behavior with people who are just like you. I am a white, professional female in my 50s with brown hair and green eyes. I can connect with other people like me very easily. There isn't anything wrong with that except that it's a very small part of what the world has to offer and it's risky because we can falsely feel like we are engaged without making any effort to connect to and celebrate God's complete creation. Honestly, compared to most people I meet, I find myself to be quite boring. I love peeking at life through someone else's eyes and discovering perspectives I never knew existed.

• Keep it simple. You don't need an elaborate greeting. "Hello," "good morning," "good evening" all work beautifully when shared with warmth. If you start to feel pretty good about your 15-5 skills and want to take it to the next level, try this. Make an observation and offer a compliment to the guest, "Good morning, I love your shoes" can work wonders on a weary soul working their way through a distracting day. Of course, find a sincere compliment and make a real observation. One happy consequence, if you can get comfortable enough to try this, the return on investment, as far as responses to your greetings, multiplies.

• For multiple safety reasons and so that you don't miss out on the joy of connecting with others, keep your phone down when walking or waiting. It will not kill you to wait for someone or something without looking at your phone. It's become a habit to pull out a phone rather than look around when we are waiting for anything. Break the habit, keep watch, engage, practice your 15-5 skills, and enjoy the space and opportunities that waiting presents.

In the book of Revelation Chapter 3 verse 2, we read the message, "Be watchful, and strengthen the things which remain, that are ready to

Hospitality and the Holy Spirit

die, for I have not found your works perfect before God." Let's be careful and make sure that we don't allow human engagement to become something that is "ready to die." Understanding and practicing the 15-5 rule is a great exercise for a youth group, a congregation, a business looking to improve their customer experience, a school group or anyone looking to bring more hospitality into their life. This is what genuine hospitality looks and feels like. Anyone can do it.

Dear Lord, Please help me get out of my own way,
keep my eyes up and capture the moments that are part of today.
Help me to be "mostly sunny" even when clouds enter
my mind and my mood. Amen.

Tips to Improve Hospitality in Your Home, Church, or Business

- Practice the 15-5 rule and teach it to someone else
- Smells matter. Don't leave the scent to chance. Be deliberate with the scents you choose to support the environment you wish to create. As a sense, smell is powerful and dominant. Be sure it is working for you, not against you.
- Be "other's centered" and interested versus interesting. Focus your attention on the needs and desires of your guest, visitor, or customer. Focus intently on creating something for them, not you. Walk through the experience from your guest's perspective and identify the opportunities to create meaningful connections.
- Eliminate distractions and clutter. Simple, clean, easy to navigate environments allow for the best human interactions.
- The goodbye matters. Our final experience carries a more lasting impression than our initial experience. Don't underestimate the value of or miss this opportunity to show you care, say thank you, or invite someone to return.

About the Author

A fast-paced gate, encouraging smile, people-centered focus, and "GO FOR IT" attitude. . . it must be Denise Maiatico, Vice President Meyer Jabara Hotels.

It would not be accurate to say one works *for* Denise. It is more appropriate to say each works *with* Denise. She is a hands-on leader who is skilled at setting the vision and empowering the team, but she is also willing to roll up her sleeves and wash dishes, turn rooms, set an event, and greet guests with the best of them.

Denise graduated from the Indiana University of Pennsylvania in 1991 with a Bachelor's Degree in Communication. She began more than twenty years ago with Meyer Jabara Hotels starting as Regional Sales Director for five properties. She was then promoted to the General Manager of the Courtyard Marriott Lehigh Valley/I-78. Her team opened the 138-room hotel and became a trusted hospitality provider with intense loyalty. Then, she took on the challenge of opening the state-of-the-art 124-room Hyatt Place Bethlehem and successfully positioned the property as a new hotel in historic Bethlehem. The guests continue to rave about the experience.

Denise's Lehigh Valley roots serve her well now as the Vice President for the region and yet another property.

Denise loves learning and teaching, and she enjoys her additional role as Adjunct Professor of Hospitality at Northampton Community College. She has received numerous sales and leadership awards from various community organizations, Meyer Jabara Hotels and the brands Marriott, Hyatt, and Holiday Inn. Denise was recognized as a Lehigh Valley Woman of Influence in 2013, as the Outstanding Businesswoman of the Year by the Bethlehem Chamber in 2013, and under her leadership, MJ hotels of the Lehigh Valley was nominated as Corporate Citizen of the Year in 2015. Denise was recognized by Hotel Management as one of their "37 GMs to Watch" in 2018. She loves to serve, and she sits on several boards throughout the Lehigh Valley.

Denise is enjoying her continuing study of the Bible.